GET LOCAL TRAFFIC NOW!
7 STRATEGIES WITH
4 POWER DRIVEN FACTORS
-- REVEALED --

Today, Only Fast, Relevant, & Engaging Content WINS! Start With A Responsive Mobile Friendly Website Then Boost To Win With Nitro Tactics!

By: Suzette Helaine Kooyman

EnhanceYour.Net

EnhanceYour.Net

ISBN-13: 978-1511700917

This publication is designed to provide general information regarding the subject matter covered. However, laws and practices often vary from state to state and country to country are subject to change. Because each factual situation is different, specific advice should be tailored to the particular circumstances. For this reason, the reader is advised to consult with an advisor regarding that individual's specific situation.

The author has taken reasonable precautions in the preparation of this book and believes that the facts as presented in this work are accurate as of the date written. However, neither the author nor the publisher assumes any responsibility for any errors or omissions. The author specifically disclaims any liability resulting from the use or application of the information contained in this book, and the information is not intended to serve as legal advice related to individual situations. Enhance Your Net focuses on total market domination for their clients to set them apart in their area and elevate their status as an industry expert and obvious choice for service.

If you are ready to take your practice to the next level, visit our website at EnhanceYour.Net and register an in depth marketing analysis for your business.

Table of Contents

Why It's Getting Harder To Get New Customers

Local businesses are seeing more competition for customers, clients, and clients than ever before. A recent Small Business Administration study reports that local businesses are seeing the largest increase in years.

Since 1990, large corporations have eliminated 4 million jobs and local businesses have added 8 million new jobs. The number of local businesses has increased 49% since 1982... that is nearly 12 million new businesses that are all competing for customers.

But it Gets Worse!

Recent statistics show that even after coming out of the hard economic times of the past several years, many local businesses are struggling to survive and many will go out of business in the next 3-5 years.

To make matters worse, recent statistics show that most local businesses are relying on traditional methods of getting clients and those methods have stopped working...

Good News: There Are Still Plenty of Customers Out There!

It's true and I can tell you that if you are ready to take your business to the next level, the information I am about to share could be worth a fortune to you!

The good news is that it is very likely that you will be able to implement these strategies without having to spend any more than you already are on advertising. (Don't worry if you aren't spending any money on advertising I will show you very low-cost effective ways to get your message in front of people hungry for your product or service)

New Customer Getting Methods

So how do you get more customers? Of course there is traditional advertising, cold calling, networking etc. But these are the things that most businesses have been doing from the start and so has the competition.

We need to breathe some fresh air into this area of your business. There are actually 34 methods that can be leveraged to get more clients, but that would probably overwhelm most business owners and I want to give you a few of the most effective ways so you can start and get some success under your belt.

Here is the initial list I work from for my consulting clients:

- ***Search Engine Optimization***
- Google Adwords
- Social Media Marketing
- ***Online Directories***

- ***Mobile Marketing***
- YouTube Marketing
- ***LinkedIn***
- Direct Response Marketing
- Power Referrals
- Trade Publications
- Trade Show Marketing
- Direct Mail

Whew... Big Sigh... That's a lot of stuff to jump on right out of the gate... I thought you said just a few. Well the fact is that is we will only look at less than half of the methods.

Let's look at a few that you can implement and get some quick momentum, no matter what type of business you have.

It doesn't matter if you are selling a physical product, a service or an information product the methods I am about to share will work for you!

Spreading the Word About Your Business!

If you look at traditional advertising like Yellow Pages, the newspaper or TV commercials these platforms all have one thing in common. They are expensive and there is no real way to measure their effectiveness.

Let's look first at the Yellow Pages... let me ask you a question...

Do you know where your yellow pages book is right now? My hallucination is that you don't, as a matter of fact you may not even have one in your office. When was the last time you looked in the yellow pages for a business? If you are like me, it was a few years ago.

Even though this is commonplace, many businesses still spend thousands each year on yellow page ads. Studies show that the average age of a person who uses yellow pages is over 70 years of age... So if this is not your target market... then you marketing dollars may be more effective with newer methods.

I look at TV commercials and Newspaper ads as a place where you spend money telling people all about your product or service and hope they either need it at the exact moment they see the advertisement or remember your ad when they do need your service.

If you are a business owner and have ever participated in placing print ads in a paper you were probably told, if the rep had your best interest in mind, that you need to publish at least seven times before you can expect to see any kind of result. Results usually start at exposure eight and beyond before any kind of real attention happens. Having been on both sides of the fence so to speak I can confirm this.

Even if you have the same exact ad that started small and got bigger over at least seven times you would have a much greater impact then to do one big ad six times.

Most business papers that have a local focus by city or suburb tends to run only once to maybe twice a month. They promote that because of the infrequent circulation that people tend to hold onto it longer. They might be true but how many times will you read a paper? Even if it was weekly just think of how long you are dragging out your sales cycle for those clients you did get. That alone is costly!

Here is a question about the newspaper...Do you get the local paper on a daily basis?

Again, my guess is probably not, and it is a safe guess because 24 of the top 25 newspapers have seen record declines in sales. I would also venture to guess that if you do place ads in the newspaper you can't tell me where I should look to find information about your business... that's because even though ads pay for the lion's share of the newspaper's publishing costs... they get placed where ever there is space left after the articles are all laid out for maximum readership.

So when it comes to print you are much better off to either get an article printed (because its news – people read it more often) or have some sort of media piece put into place where the reporter of that segment can highlight you in one of their articles. This is best because its someone else talking about you.

Also if you choose to do an article I would also strongly suggest that you do some kind of event right after within a week or two and build on it through both your website engagement, radio, and through the local specialty online calendar that hosted the article.

You can generally post events and business listings free even if you have not posted an article or ad and could be a good follow up sequence to your article. Both of those article approaches have a much higher chance of getting read and standing out over a simple new paper ad that says buy me. So unless of course you want to run non-stop ads like that of the car dealerships. Know that it can take a time to gain momentum and it's very easy to lose momentum.

Then when it comes to TV Commercials not only is it almost impossible to measure effectiveness, most people watch recorded shows these days and skip the commercials all together. So what is a business owner to do?

Start of a New Era: How the Internet Became Local

Businesses of all types and scopes are just starting to become aware of what a small percentage of early adopters already know: Internet and mobile device platforms have revolutionized marketing.

Thanks to high-speed wireless networks, mobile devices, communications software, and social platforms, marketing has been transformed into a largely digital discipline for local businesses.

This new media is quickly replacing old school advertising methods such as newspaper ads, printed business directories like the Yellow Pages, direct mail coupons—even radio and TV ads.

Online marketing is also effective whether or not a business currently sells products or services over the Internet. "Brick and mortar" businesses of all kinds are using these new strategies with impressive results.

Local consumers increased usage of the Internet and mobile media is driving businesses to learn how to take advantage of these new platforms so their prospects and customers can find them, hear about them and, ultimately, buy from them.

This is also important because the Internet is now interactive. Consumers are sharing their experiences with local businesses... Both positive and negative! Not only is it very important for business owners to know to control the message that they're putting out, but they must also keep track of what people are saying about their business.

Take a look at the statistics: Google has over 3.5 billion searches every day; out of those 3.5 billion searches over 28 billion a month (equivalent to 27% of all searches) are local. What that means is people are actually putting in a geographic identifier in the search bar.

For instance if you're in Salt Lake City and you're looking

for a dentist, chances are you don't just put in "dentist"; chances are you put in "dentist" or "Salt Lake City dental office." You type something that identifies where you are geographically.

From there the search engine knows to go find the information that's most relevant for you. After all, if you have a toothache, you don't really care about how great the dentist in Seattle is if you live in Salt Lake City. The same thing goes for a pizza joint. If you're looking for pizza, you probably aren't looking for just pizza in general; you're looking for it based on where you're located.

Here's another amazing statistic: 82% of local searches are followed by an action, a store visit, a call, an email or a purchase. So when people are searching locally, it means they're ready to take an action and more likely to buy. They are a purchase driven consumer!

Gaining Local Market Share:
Capitalizing on Local Searches

The great news is there are a number of ways that we can put information online for people to find when they're searching locally. Local Internet marketing is based on helping local business owners put information online where people can find it at the exact time that they're looking for it. That's very important and it's very different than other forms of advertising.

For instance, look at the yellow pages. Stop and ask yourself this question: do you know where your phone book is right now? Probably not... If you're like 80% of the population, you don't have a clue where that giant book is. The average age of someone who uses yellow pages is over 70 years of age. This means if a business is in the yellow pages alone, they are missing out on the vast majority of the population.

Remember the Internet uses a technological way of finding the most relevant information about businesses, and nearly everyone uses it. Old school methods just don't produce enough results to even pay for themselves anymore.

Alternatively local Internet marketing provides a strategy for local businesses to put their information in hundreds of places so that people can find the information at exact time that they need the product or service.

Both in theory and in practice, this has proven to be a much better solution and makes it much easier for the business owner to see the value of their advertising funds rather than just continuing to spend thousands of dollars on ineffective means of marketing.

Preselling Your Business Online– Building a Great Website to Kick Start Your Internet Marketing Plan

Preselling your business online is important; in order to make it work, you'll need a great website. In fact, a robust site can actually be the key to the beginning of your internet marketing campaign. When you begin looking at the task of promotion, it helps to understand what all is involved in the process. You want to generate highly targeted, qualified customers. To do this, you'll need a great-looking, functional website that will garner traffic.

There are several aspects that make up a successful Internet marketing plan. They should be the building blocks of your campaign. You need to generate interest. Knowing what your target audience wants is the key to giving them content that will be of interest to them. Since you are marketing via the Internet, you'll be selling the idea of your business to visitors who are seeking the type of information you have to offer. This can serve you well because it takes the guesswork out of figuring out what they need to know. You'll need to include this information on your website. It should be informative and easy to read.

Educate your visitors. Give them something they can use. Instead of just recycling the same information found on other similar websites, make yours unique. Tell your visitors something that will be relevant and important. This is what will keep them coming back time after time.

Create desire. A well-built website should give them the desire to want to know more. Keep the content interesting and fresh. Include any new information relevant to the topics pertaining to services offered by your vein clinic.

When you presell your business online, you are preparing your prospects for what is offered on your website. Email marketing is also a great way to get prospects to your site. While the website itself is the starting point for your internet marketing plan, the emails you send will be used to entice people into becoming visitors.

Take the Avatar approach to

Marketing

Know your market. When you understand who you are talking to, knowing what to tell them will be easier. Your website (and all communication as far as that goes) should be based on your target market. Consider who will likely visit your website. Ask yourself what they will want to know.

All too often a business owner will mistakenly try to take a "talk to the masses" approach to marketing be it online or off. This is a big – big mistake!

Taking that kind of approach is like taking a mudslinging approach to marketing - throwing mud on a wall and see what sticks. What happens? If the mud is too wet you'll have a big muddy glob that hits the wall and falls off right? Then you might even get a few of the less condensed versions of mud pellets that will stick for a short time then dry up and fall off. This approach again increases your bounce rate and drops your overall ranking score.

Frequently this can be caused by using to general of and highly competitive keyword searches. Sure it might be grabbing everyone's attention but it's just enough for them to say, "Hugh, that's not what I want!" and off they go. This can also be costly if you are running any kind of paid advertising. So now it has negatively affected your *SEO* efforts and advertising dollars.

So what do you do? Create Avatars for your business. This would be best explained using the services of a dentist. What types of services does a typical dentist offer?

Tooth cleaning, whitening, filling - **Preventative Care.**
But they also offer Root Canals, Bridge work, dentures – **Restorative services.**
Implants – Veneers – **Cosmetic services.**

They might even break out their services by age for a more refined niche. Using tag lines like "Small Hands for a Small Mouth." For a pediatric dentist. Or something else for adult or elderly focused because each segment would require some sort of tweaking. This approach lets them know that you are interested in them and not just their pocket book right?

So in this scenario you are talking to at least three very different clients with different needs and possibly even six or more if they do specialty work by age or gender. Remember people want to be talked **with not to** and as that of a person not a number. So to accomplish this create an actual avatar for each segment that you work with and give them a name! Post it in front of you when you are writing copy of any kind for them.

HOT TIP: Create an avatar – give them a name and list their characteristics under their name as a reminder. Look at the sample avatars below and experience how much easier it is to write with a face in mind.

This is great to use in all areas of your marketing, blog, and ads. Especially in social media marketing. Another benefit of doing this creates "stickiness." In other words, the reader will be more interested in what you have to say when it has been written with them in mind and will stay on your site longer.

Use examples or scenarios on your website. This gives your readers something to relate to in a very direct way. If what you wrote describes that person, you have just come that much closer to gaining a customer. This allows you to create the needed interest that will draw your prospect closer.

Include different scenarios. Not all your prospects will be in the same situation. In fact, some may be very different. You can appeal to a wider range of clients by including a number of scenarios.

Make sure the information on your site is clear. Your readers should have no problem understanding your information. Use language that makes sense to the masses. If you must use industry jargon, be sure to explain it. Only use industry language when necessary. Otherwise, explain things in terms that are easy to comprehend. You want your customers to relate to you on a very personal level. This is what will cause a peak in their interest and keep them coming back.

Converting Website Visitors to Buyers

The key to a successful website is conversion. You ultimately want those who visit your website to become a paying customer. You will need a plan of action in order to make this happen. This plan will enable you to build relationships and create the trust necessary to increase the number of visitors you receive, but to also make them stay. Below are tips that will show you how to implement a site designed with conversion in mind.

Provide quality content about the products and services offered at your business. Make sure it is clear and concise. Information that is easy to understand will appeal to visitors, especially those who are conducting an initial search. Grab your visitor's attention immediately. This means putting the most important information first. Think of the main points you want them to be aware of and make sure these are incorporated before everything else.

Create a website that is easy to navigate. Confusing layouts or content that is difficult to follow will prompt visitors to go elsewhere for information. Write all content with your potential clients in mind. Explain what you can do for them and how helpful your services will be. List the benefits of your services and tell them why they should choose your business.

Design your website specific for the target audience. This means creating each page with respective types of visitors in mind. For example, you might link a specific page to a particular ad. That page might contain information about the services you offer. So, if a visitor is searching specifically for this type of information, it needs to be very easily accessible so clients can reach it both quickly and easily. This will take the guesswork out of navigating the entire site just to find the information they want.

On the other hand, another visitor might be reading an article about the benefits of your products and services and see a direct link to your home page. That person isn't necessarily looking for a specific type of information, but rather is searching for something more general. It's all about directing visitors to the right site, and you can use your various advertising mediums to target specific pages.

Implement active thinking... Use an active voice in all your content to keep your visitors motivated. Your copy should be engaging and make them want to continue reading. This is a more dynamic approach and often makes people feel as if they are being spoken to directly. It helps establish a rapport, which can quickly lead to a conversion.

Increase the trust between you and your visitors. Trust is the basis of any good relationship, and when it comes to promoting your business, it will serve you well. You want your prospects to believe in you and feel confident about the services you provide.

An effective website begins with a successful online marketing plan. Your business will greatly benefit from well-thought out pages designed specifically with your target market in mind. Use the tips above to build a website that will help your business grow.

The Top Five Benefits of Having a Great Website

A great website is the most important online marketing tool you can have for your business. It's where much of the relevant information will be located and is your direct link to potential prospects. There are several benefits to having a well-developed site. Below are five of the most important advantages and why they are relevant:

Benefit #1

A great website is essential, it has become a requirement of sorts. Customers expect and look for it. They want to know there is a specific place they can go to get information.

If you fail to establish an Internet presence, your competition will beat you in the online marketing department. Your site can make you stand out from the rest. It should depict who your business is. Tell readers about the services you offer and how they can contact you. Your website should be informative and easy to read and navigate.

Benefit #2

A great website helps build trust. It shows your visitors you have something important to offer and gives them a place to go where they can learn more. Here is where you will have the chance to build your online image. It also shows your expertise in the field.

Benefit #3

A great website increases the odds of others learning about your business. Now that many people are turning to the Internet for obtaining information, it is being relied upon to produce results. These results are produced by search engines.

The ultimate goal is to receive high rankings for all your pages. The more individual pages that rank high on your site, the more visible you'll be online. For this, *search engine optimization* (*SEO*) is key. The content of your *website should incorporate keywords potential clients* will use to find you. A well optimized site will place you high in the rankings.

Benefit #4

Design your site carefully. While you definitely want to keep the content easy to read and navigate, all your pages should be eye-catching. Many people choose a particular theme for their site. This helps give it a uniform look throughout.

Choose a theme or look that is relevant to what you are offering. Consider usability while making sure the content and all elements will grab the attention of visitors. A well-designed site that is easy to navigate and contains useful information will prompt them to stay.

Benefit #5

A great website will give a great first impression. This is very important, especially to those who are hearing of you for the first time online. You need pages that look professional, are user-friendly, and will provide your potential customers with everything they'll need to begin taking advantage of your services.

Always include up-to-date information. This is absolutely essential. A site that hasn't been updated in a while will detract from your credibility in the eyes of visitors. You want it to look like there's been activity and you want that activity to be real. Add some useful articles or blog posts. This will show that you visit the site frequently and are in touch with the needs of your clients.

Make sure all contact information is correct. Visitors who are unable to make contact with questions will often go elsewhere. You can avoid this by providing several ways in which they may get in touch. Your website will serve you well if it receives the right attention. Think of it as a part of your overall business and allow it to grow with you.

Why Great Website Copy Is Essential

Your website should contain great website copy for several reasons. Presenting information the right way is what will get you high search engines rankings. These high rankings are what will enable people to find you. If you rank near (or at) the top, you will receive more hits than if you rank in the middle or the bottom. Many web users often don't make it very far down a results page before trying a new search. Most people don't like to search through hundreds of results and simply don't do it. That is why having a high website ranking is crucial. You want to be seen at the top.

The key is getting several pages to rank high. This allows you to take up several of the spots near the top. This will result in your name and URL being seen multiple times. Users will often click on a name they repeatedly see.

Great website copy presents a call to action. It clearly informs the user of what to do. For example, you might include a page on your website listing the benefits your services provide to your customers. This should be done in such a way that will prompt them to contact you to learn more. If the benefits are listed very clearly on your page, they should be easy to understand. The same is true for whatever action you want them to take.

Great web copy also evokes emotion. You want your visitors to feel something when they go to your site. Many may not be familiar with exactly what services you offer, and upon finding out, may feel a particular emotion. Perhaps it's hope or maybe even excitement because they finally have found the information they need. No matter what it is, you have made a difference. While it is about what you say, it's also about how you say it.

Your web copy should also tell compelling stories. These can come in the form of testimonials. People often respond well upon hearing about the experiences of others. You might even explain why you decided to open your business and tell readers about your expertise in the field.

When writing your copy, tell your stories in a way that will speak directly to your visitors. This is one of the easiest ways to turn a prospect into a customer. This is also a great way to gain trust. Prospects will want to come to you if they feel you know what you are doing and will take good care of them.

Your website copy is what will help establish your online credibility. You must write content that will inform, convince, identify with your visitor, and inspire a particular action to be taken. This often leads to the sharing of such information. A visitor who has become a customer may then recommend others to visit your website and, ultimately, your business. Your online presence should expand your business. It can help you reach people who aren't in close proximity to you, but who might greatly benefit from the services you have to offer.

Getting Traffic to Your Business: Tools Needed To Get Started With Local Online Marketing

There are 7 major strategies for creating a dominating local online presence. We will discuss each in great detail in the following chapters. When properly executed each of the strategies can bring new customers to your local business. When you combine these strategies you create a formidable presence for your business.

There is also four power driven factors that will be revealed in the pages that follow. When you implement these four factors to their fullest extent into these seven strategies you can literally turbo boost the results of your marketing efforts. Like in the movie called "The Fast and Furious" when two leading cars are neck in neck and approaching the finish line they kick in the nitro (a special fuel component) for a Turbo boost to WIN!

Throughout this book, I have italicized and bolded the key word or phrase pertaining to the power driven factors. This was done so as not to take away from the current topic or strategy being discussed while helping you to embed their importance.

In some cases, I have elaborated on that key factor for a better understanding. Where it is warranted, I have pointed you to a resource for additional training. Mastering the scope of these power factors can turbo boost your results!

I have also added in some **"HOT TIPS"** along the way for you to be able to maximize your result for that particular area.

Let's get started!

Strategy #1: Search Engine Optimization - Ensuring Your Page Ranking

Search Engine Optimization (*SEO*) makes a website more desirable to the search engines. The main ways to optimize a website are through creating great content, specific keywords that are searched for on a regular basis, interaction on your website from people visiting and you also want to have other sites pointing to your website (which is called back linking).

When Google or one of the other search engines crawls (looks at) a website and it sees that there are other reputable websites (referred to as authority sites) that have links pointing to your website, they go, "Hey, other sites think this is important, so this site must be important," and it moves the site up the search rankings. The other important key is to have links out to other high-ranking authority sites like CNN, YouTube, etc. When the search engines see that your site is pointing to some of these other high ranking sites that have great information it helps to move your site up in the rankings.

The other part about *SEO* is using keywords. What are the words that you want to show up for when people are searching? When it comes to local marketing, it's not as hard as you may think. You can ask the first 10 people you run into, "If you were looking for a dentist in Salt Lake City, what would you type in to the search bar?" More than likely if you ask 10 people, their search phrase in the search bar would probably be about the same as the question that you just asked them. Remember people think and talk like a person. So should you for a better result. Google will figure out the key words that they are stating.

With local marketing that's about as complicated as you need to get with keyword research. Now, there are a lot of tools out there that can go very in-depth but I would say you could very easily use the keyword tool that's available in any search engine to look at how many searches people are actually doing and how strong the competition is.

Previously the majority of website rankings were based on technical attributes. Things like On-page **SEO**, overuse of keywords (keyword stuffing), backlinks etc. previously helped your websites ranking. Now Content Creation is King. Google is now friendlier to original content than purchased traffic. The search engines use an ever-changing algorithm to determine what shows up on the first page. Today they reward originality of quality content and visitor interaction (time on site) more so than the number of backlinks.

HOT TIP: Having a blog on the same domain name on i.e. *Mobile or Responsive web design* helps with engagement with fresh content. Plus set the video on auto play to grab attention.

Also in regards to FaceBook it too is constantly changing its algorithms and requirements. Recently they started to require photos and video to be hosted on a secured (SSL) Certificate site for security reasons as opposed to a non-secured. There is a bigger benefit to this though. Because you can convert any youtube video to MP4 version and host it on your *responsive web design* so that it automatically resizes with the device used and the viewer doesn't get distracted with other videos that will pop up in an embed from Youtube.

KeyWord Research – What Are Your Prospects Looking For?

Keywords are the foundation of *SEO*. Keywords are the exact terms consumers are using to find what they are searching for. Single keywords are too broad of a search term for local searches. Three to Five words together are known as "long tail keyword phrases" are more powerful for local searches since they usually include a geographic identifier. These are usually used for very specific searches and have higher conversions.

Optimizing your website with long tail keywords is very important. By placing 4 to 6 long tail keywords in your website's code and in the page titles can help your websites ranking. An example of a single keyword would be the term "marketing". An example of a long tail keyword would be "Social Media Marketing Salt Lake City, UT". As you can tell someone using the single keyword is looking for general information on marketing. The person using the long tail keyword phrase is going to find specific results for the social media marketing agencies in Salt Lake City, UT.

When creating content for Facebook, Twitter, blogs, YouTube, etc. always use your keywords in the title first. Content Creation with relevant keywords will help your website's organic ranking, and remember to avoid overstuffing. Overstuffing is excessive use of keywords and is frowned upon by search engines.

A great way to find out the best keywords to use for your website or content is by using Google's free keyword tool. You can research your specific keywords and it will make suggestions of keyword terms that are closely related to your search terms.

The keyword planner will show you how many searches each term gets per month over the last six month span. This can help you identify the best terms to use so that the most targeted people will see your information. It will also show you which keywords are rated low, medium and highly competitive and give you an idea of how much your ad could cost. This is important because it will be easier to rank for the low to medium competition keywords which will not only gets you a better result but a more cost effective when you apply paid traffic as a strategy.

Why Mobilegeddon? - Google's Impending Doom On All Sites That Are Not Mobile Friendly.

April 21, 2015 will mark one of the most devastating days in *SEO* history for those who have chosen to turn a blind eye to this hammer that Google is imposing on your non-mobile websites. Hence, the phrase **"Go Mobile or Get Crushed!** Becomes a reality!

We've just covered the importance of *SEO* and how it helps you get found via nationally or better yet locally with proper *SEO*. Some of you have worked hard to get your rankings on Google and it probably has been costly either in the costs of getting it done or even more costly in profits if you haven't.

For those of you who have built a strong online presence if you have not gone mobile by the deadline you are looking to lose up to at least 50% of your ranking status according to Google who manages that through algorithms and such. Are you seriously going to just let this new algorithm *bleed out your SEO PROFITS?* I would hope not! For some that could cause a business to go under over night!

Google in 2013 claimed 67% of all search market that made it the most popular worldwide! So when Google speaks it is **wise** to <u>listen</u> – <u>pay attention</u> and – most of all <u>**ACT**</u> on their information. Google is all about granting the best user experience providing them with the most relevant data and ease of use. Hence their intensive research that they have put into what device(s) the user is pulling the data from.

In fact, they are so serious about it that it was the first time ever that they actually sent out direct emails and other communications through the use of web master tools notifications to a large majority of web masters. Telling the web masters about the change that was going to happen with a set date.

The reason why this is so remarkable is because for years Google never released a date of algorithms. Instead the anticipated dates would be revealed by the media and would eventually be confirmed by the action taking place.

Here is the link for the Google Web Master Central blog. **http://googlewebmastercentral.blogspot.com/2015/0 2/finding-more-mobile-friendly-search.html** The following information was posted: Thursday, February 26, 2015 where Google announced two things. Effective that day of posting they were starting to use:

"2. More relevant app content in search results

Starting today, we will begin to use information from indexed apps ***as a factor in ranking*** for signed-in users who have the app installed. As a result, we may now surface content from indexed apps more prominently in search."

So the take away, just having a mobile site is not the only means of ranking your business. Having a custom app in place can help tremendously. This is especially true for local searches and real-time engagement with

your site – preferably mobile site for a positive impact.

Look at what else Google said:

"1. More mobile-friendly websites in search results

Starting April 21, we will be expanding our use of mobile-friendliness as a ranking signal. This change will affect mobile searches in all languages worldwide and _**will have a significant impact in our search results.**_ Consequently, users will find it easier to get relevant, high quality search results that are optimized for their devices."

There is also another reason behind this change that is favorable to Google. That's because a responsive web design has a fluid grid which means only one HTML code and URL throughout the site. So it makes it easier for the bots to complete the indexing of the site. In addition to that when a company has two sites one is mobile and the other is a desktop the bots have to index the same information twice. It also leads to greater costs for the business owner because due to the different URL's you have to run separate SEO campaigns.

Another added costs for the business owner when they have a mobile and desktop version of their site is that it is costing them potential customers in the social media aspect.

Why's that you say? Here's why.

Let's say that you have posted some awesome content on your mobile version that someone wants to share. When that person shares that info on social media and another person opens up that sharing on a desktop version they are not going to get the same optimized version that the first person saw to be so awesome. When that happens they bounce out. This results in a backfire. Because now instead of the viewer being excited about what they saw they get disappointed and you lose that potential client to the next website.

So there you have it, three different perspectives from Google, the end user and your pocketbook as the affected business owner to the importance of having a *responsive web design*. It's imperative to have.

Strategy #2: Pay Per Click – Google AdWords… and Yahoo & Bing

Advertising on Google is done by placing your ads in front of people who are actively searching for a term or "keyword phrase" also known as a "long tail" that is related to your product of service.

You are charged each time someone clicks on your ad. When they click on your ad it takes them to the web page you want them to see that will lead them to an engagement and making a purchase from you.

Let's look at an example of a company in Greenville that sells Pool Supplies. They want their ads to show up in front of people who are actively searching for information about "pool supplies" and probably lives in Greenville. We don't know exactly what type of information they are looking for, we just know they are they are searching the term "Greenville Pool Supplies".

The ads show up at the Top of the Results page and along the right hand side of the page similar to Facebook ads. The results in the middle of the page are organic search results. These are important but we will save that for a different time.

When someone gets the result for searching "Greenville Pool Supplies" they have the option of clicking on the links that most appeal to them. There is no guarantee that your ad will get clicked, you have to have a great headline, and body content that intrigues the prospect. But at least by adding the long tail phrase you just increased your chances of at least being seen as an option.

The 7 Steps to Set Up a Winning AdWords Campaign

#1 - Set Your Goals

You will want to determine exactly what you're looking to achieve with your campaign. Do you want a specific number of leads per month? Are you looking to increase inbound phone calls, newsletter signups, or make sales on your web site?

#2 - Do Your Research

Research the Keywords – Use keyword tools like Market Samurai or Google's Keyword Planner to find the most relevant keywords people are typing into the search engines to find your product/service/company.

Research Your Competition – You will want to spend some time looking at the competition to see who consistently is ranking at or near the top of the rankings (you can use a spy tool like Keyword Spy Tool to help). Pay attention to their ad copy and offers. Visit their websites. Sign up for their mailing lists. Purchase their products.

Research Your Audience – Where are customers buying and reviewing products/services/businesses like yours online? Take a look at the reviews they are posting.

What do they love/hate about your competition? What are the needs or desires they're looking to fulfill? While doing this part of the research you should be on the lookout for great quotes you can use for ad copy.

#3 The Landing Page/Offer

An irresistible offer on your landing page it the absolute keystone to your AdWords campaign. While you were doing your research you saw what all your top competitors are offering. Now all you have to do is make your offer just a little bit unique, different, or better. It is amazing what just a small improvement over the competition here can make!

#4 Use Exact Match Keywords

When first starting out with AdWords, you will want your keyword list very small (5 – 10 keywords) and very focused (the ones that people who are ready to buy are most likely to be typing into Google). Add all these keywords to your campaign as Exact Match keywords (this means that your ads will only be shown when someone types that exact term into Google). This way your ads will only show up for the most relevant searches and not for variations that Google may think are relevant, but aren't.

Over time, you can eliminate the keywords that aren't getting clicks/conversions and expand on the ones that are.

For example, if "Salt Lake City Dentist" is working for you, add more Exact Match variations of it to the list. Do this by combining the word "dentist" with zip codes, nearby cities, and by using variations like "dentists near Salt Lake City, UT", "best dentist in Salt Lake City", etc.

#5 Use Unique and Proven Ads

The ad copy should be highly relevant to the keywords they show up for (including the exact terms when possible). Make sure you stand out from the competition by using different offers, benefits, etc. Your landing page/offer should also reflect the same messaging as your ads to help people feel they are in the right place. (If your landing page is not consistent with your ad copy it will hurt your conversions.

Test your ads. To do this you will place at least 2 ads in each ad group and then split test them. As a general rule of thumb, after each ad has at least 30 clicks, delete the lower performing ad and replace it with a new one.

HOT TIP: When doing a split test just change one aspect at a time to measure your results and segregate when possible!

Having two or more differences will water down your results and cost money due to the inability to narrow the key producing factors. In FaceBook, you have the capability to segregate your target market even more by separating the results based upon age, gender, and other demographics. The results can truly help you determine where you should be putting your marketing dollars.

#6 Track Your Results

Whatever the goals for your campaign, track your results. Track downloads, newsletter signups, sales, etc. with AdWords conversion tracking. If phone calls are what you're after, use a Call Tracking service.

#7 Mine the Data

You get data from AdWords you can't get anywhere else. Take advantage of it.

You can use the keyword data to find keywords that are good candidates for *Search Engine Optimization* (*SEO*) for your website.

As mentioned above, test different messages, headlines and offers in your ads. When you find the ones that people really respond to, test them on your landing pages and in other marketing media.

Used this way the information you get from AdWords
and Facebook Ads can be the grease that lubes your
entire marketing engine.

Strategy #3: Local Online Directories – Placing Your Business In Your Prospects Pockets

Local directories are web properties that allow businesses to list the details of their business at no cost. These directories can be vitally important for any local businesses. These listings can show up in the online search results and on apps on mobile phones like CitySearch, Google Maps, Yelp, and many more.

The reason this is critical for any local business is that according to a comScore-Localeze survey, 50% of Local Searches on mobile devices are done using these *Directory Apps.* It's like every person with a smart phone is walking around with access to 15 different phone books at their disposal at any second, right in the palm of their hand!

So which one is it most important to be listed in?...

*The simple answer is **<u>all of them</u>**!*

You may have heard of ***Google+*** Local because it is the largest local ***directory*** on the Internet. It actually gives information for local business as a listing in Google. This allows clients a way to actually show up on the first page of Google whenever someone searches for their industry and city. If you put in "Salt Lake City Dentist," as I mentioned earlier, it will show up with dentists in Salt Lake City that are on a map shown on Google.

Simply put: ***Google+*** Local is the way for any local business to put information online and have it show up on the first page. As a matter of fact, there are businesses who don't even have a website who have first page Google listings because they have put the correct information on their ***Google+*** page.

Many business owners are not as familiar with ***Google+*** as they are with other social media websites. However, with approximately 343 million active users, the site is gaining in popularity and should be considered as part of your marketing plan.

One of the most popular aspects of *Google+* is that it allows users to create circles. These circles can include friends, businesses, work colleagues, and customers. By creating different circles for each of these groups, you can then share specific information with a specific circle.

This technique allows you to create customer and business related content that you can then share in the respective circle. This is a great way for businesses to tailor their marketing plan to reach their target market using *Google+*.

Another benefit that *Google+* has to offer is that it allows you to share coupons, announce new products, host contests, share blog posts, and publicize current promotions. This is a great way for businesses to share information that is relevant to their existing clients and helpful in attracting new ones. Businesses also have the opportunity to use their *Google+* page as a way to humanize their business. This can be done by sharing videos or stories about your employees and what they do each day.

In addition to the benefits we have already mentioned, another important benefit to using *Google+* is that it can have a positive effect on your online visibility. When people interact with your *Google+* page or +1 your content, it is demonstrating to Google that people are interested in your business. When Google notices this, they will begin to reward your activity on *Google+* with a higher search engine ranking. This means that when people search for a product or service that you offer, you will become easier to find and be placed closer to the top of the search results provided.

Another way that being an active member on *Google+* can help your business is that when your posts are properly optimized, Google will take notice. To ensure that your posts are properly optimized, you should include keywords and topics that relate to your specific business niche. When optimizing your content, it is important that you include these terms in your content naturally. If you include too many keywords, or they do not flow organically they may have the opposite effect. Keep your content natural and organic and you will get the attention of Google.

Google+ is a valuable marketing tool for any business. If you are already using social media as part of your marketing plan you should definitely consider what *Google+* has to offer. It is a great way to increase awareness about your business and attract new clients.

How to Get *Google+* Reviews for Your Business

A *Google+* listing for your business is an integral part of your internet reputation. It will be an invaluable tool for your online marketing plan. One essential factor is reviews.

Customer reviews can make or break you; they are what often provide others with the information to make a decision. You want plenty of positive reviews in order to make the most out of your *Google+* listing.

The reviews you receive should be relevant, high quality customer accounts. So how do you handle this aspect of your *Google+* listing? Below are some tips that will get you started; these tips will show you how to get reviews as well as respond to them.

Ask for positive reviews. This is simple. If you have satisfied customers, encourage them to visit your *Google+* listing and write a review. Explain how easy it is to do and won't take very long. They will only need to click on the "write a review" button located at the top left corner of your listing and begin typing.

Google+ provides you with a link that is personalized just for your business. You can send it to your email and/or regular postal mail lists for the purpose of directing people to your listing. When doing this, be sure to ask for reviews. You should also include this link on all business correspondence as well as ads and marketing materials. This is another great way to promote your link and request reviews.

Generate a QR code linked to your listing. Place it on everything business related your customers may be likely to see. Include a simple request for them to post a review after visiting your listing. QR codes will take anyone accessing the internet via a smart phone directly to your *Google+* listing with a quick scan. This process is easy and effective.

List your business in **directories** such as: **Bing**, **Yelp**, and **Yahoo**. Business listings, **Foursquare**, and all other reviews that are submitted to those sites will be automatically linked to and will show up on your **Google+ listing.**

Responding to reviews is just as important as receiving them. Feedback is very important and can go both ways. Below are more useful tips. Unfortunately, there will always be people who are unhappy with your business no matter what you do. Sometimes these people will be unhappy with any business. Still, you will want to respond in a way that will preserve your reputation. Responding is the way to do this.

Respond promptly. This will show the negative reviewers you are paying attention to what they had to say. Make an attempt through your response to resolve any existing issues. Express your perspective in a way that isn't insulting or self-justifying.

You will, of course, get plenty of positive reviews. Always be sure to thank your satisfied customers for their support. In the case of your business, tell your clients how much you appreciate their great reviews. You might also offer public referral rewards and coupons to customers through the *Google Plus listing* forum. This will encourage potential customers to pay you a visit.

There are dozens of local directories available to any Local Business and in order for a listing to show up in the search results it must be consistently optimized similar to *Google+* above. Each directory listing needs to have pictures and videos. The description of the business needs to be written exactly the right way.

The features of the business and the categories all need to be listed in such a way that it gets the attention of local searchers. This allows you to show your hours of operation and directions to your location. People can push one button to call the store or get turn-by-turn directions from where they are straight to you front door.

Another powerful part of *Local Directories* are citations created by people leaving reviews of their experience with your business. Obviously, the higher the ratings and reviews, the more people like it, right? Think about the last thing you bought on Amazon, I bet you looked at the ratings other people had given the book or product before you bought. Right? The same thing goes for your local business!

Strategy #4: Social Media - Facebook, Twitter, YouTube and More

The next traffic path is social media. There are a ton of these sites on the Internet and everyone looks at Facebook and Twitter as the two biggest players online. And for good reason, Facebook has over 1 Billion users and Twitter has over 300 Million active tweeters.

These platforms provide channels for getting information in front of tons of people. You can identify them and target them locally based on the geographic information; on both of those systems, people tell you what they do, what they like and where they live (most of the time).

Facebook is more social. You can advertise and put a wider variety of information there. Twitter is about marketing to the masses and small little bursts called tweets. With Twitter, you can only post a message that's 140 characters in length. With 140 characters, you don't have a lot of room to go into a detailed description. You can target your audience with tools like twellow.com to identify people who are in the city that you're dealing with.

Facebook provides a lot more demographic information on its users, which allows you to target your audience based on location, age, gender, relationship status, education, profession, and interests. Armed with this information you can develop ad campaigns and have them presented only to your ideal client.

For instance, if you were doing a golf ad, you would definitely want to cut the demographics down to where you want it. Let's say, you wanted to target female golfers in Salt Lake City, UT. You would probably select, obviously, females. You would select a range of probably 25 to 55. You might select college educated. And you would probably select married. This should all be based on solid research on your markets demographics.

Another aspect of social media is YouTube, and I'll talk about that a little bit more when I get into the video section, but YouTube actually is a social media platform because you can have subscribers, send messages, and leave comments. So it really does become a social media platform.

LinkedIn is a social networking site designed specifically for the business community. The goal of the site is to allow registered members to establish and document networks of people they know and trust professionally. The owner of the business needs to have a *LinkedIn* profile, and the business needs to have a company profile. There are some social aspects to *LinkedIn*, but it really is about business. It's about people who are in business, business owners, salespeople, and business professionals.

The use of all of the social sites there should have a clear strategic approach in utilizing them and a scheduled engagement time. *LinkedIn*'s primary focus is in business activities where there *are a lot of untapped resources both in the program itself and in its application for networking both online and off.* Resources that the majority of professional salesmen and business owners are clueless about.

The next time that you go to a Chamber of Commerce, BNI, or some other business event do it with a purpose and not just show up with the hope of getting a lead and putting money out for an unplanned lunch or dinner. At the end of this book you will have an invitation to learn more on how to make your social connections in *LinkedIn* much more profitable then you ever thought imaginable.

Again the main goal of all these sites is to build a relationship because people don't buy from companies they buy from the people who run them. Remember people buy from those who they – Like – Know – and Trust. *LinkedIn* is a great way of doing just that and all of the sites have a great way to direct people to your website, to expedite the process. So make sure you're always leading them to both your social sites and website and incorporating some type of engagement.

On most social sites you can optimize profiles for local business. With Facebook you can set up a Facebook fan page, create a customized time line and create content for people to interact with.

For a restaurant you could post pictures of the menu items; if it's a doctor's office, you might display before and after pictures of services. You always want your posts to leave customers saying, "Wow, this is business that I feel like I know, like and trust." You want them to be a fan of the page and ultimately become a customer of the business, product or service."

You can customize the background on Twitter, customize the feed, and customize the information you provide to your followers. The information that the business owner provides should be useful to the person who's viewing it whether they choose to do business with them or not. I'll reiterate this point a few times because it really is the key factor when it comes to creating a credible presence online.

The Power of Videos

Video is one of the most powerful means of putting information online. Why? Well, ask yourself this. What do people do more often, read books or watch television? Obviously, it's watch television because most people don't want to read. They're lazy and they like to be entertained.

If you look at YouTube, what are the videos that have the most views? They're entertaining, or they're providing information. They entertain; they're funny or controversial.

Now, the other videos that get a lot of views are videos that provide great information in a way that gets people's attention. For instance, if you do a search on Google or YouTube to figure out what causes the popping sound when you crack your neck, back or knuckles, you will find a chiropractor answering the question, "What's that popping sound?" It has over 120,000 views.

That's because people want to know what that popping sound is when the chiropractor adjusts them. Whenever you answer questions that people want know, it increases the video ranking. When you post a video you want to be sure to title it with the information of how people will search for it.

For instance, going back to our "dentist in Salt Lake City" example, you would want to put "Salt Lake City Dentist Explains Why Root Canals Hurt." That way you have the **geographic identifier**, you have the **dentist (or service) part**, and then you have the **description of the content**. You also want to put in keywords and tags so that it gets people's attention and can possibly show up in the search engines.

The real value of video is having people find it in local searches, and it also provides you with tons of content that you can use to post on social media platforms.

HOT TIP: On a YouTube video you can now add into the video itself a clickable "call to action link" this link can actually take the viewer to a landing page or engage in a gaming type activity that has gotten fairly popular with YouTube. This is in addition to adding a link or call to action the description text that is placed below the video.

What we've discovered is there's a lot of different ways to make videos. You can use animoto.com where you simply put pictures in, and it'll actually add music and create a video for you. You can make videos with using PowerPoint or Keynote, which is like PowerPoint for Mac.

The simplest and easiest way to make a video is to use a very small camera (smart phone- hmmm imagine that!) and record yourself answering questions that your company get asked all time. These are called frequently asked questions. When you post these FAQ videos you will see favorable results, because people are usually looking for answers to these questions online.

Videos are very search engine friendly and can rank on the first page rather quickly with the right titling and tagging. Of course YouTube is the biggest video sharing site and the second largest search engine on the planet so it is very important to have your videos uploaded there, but YouTube is not the only player in town.

It's also very beneficial to put videos on other video sharing sites like Vimeo, Viddler, Kewego, and more. There's a ton of them out there. You can simply do a Google search for video sharing sites, and you'll get an entire list of all the places that you can post videos.

Using YouTube to Market Your Business

Getting Started – To get started using YouTube, you will first need to create your channel. This step may require a little time, but the effort you put into creating and customizing the channel to suit your business will be well worth it. When you customize your channel, you should include your logo and customize the colors to those related to your logo and business. This will give your channel a customized look and help it be recognized by those familiar with your brand. During the initial setup phase, you should include the option of allowing users to subscribe to your channel. This will ensure that your target market is receiving your latest videos.

Types of Videos – Now that you've created your channel, you're probably wondering what types of videos to begin posting. The best types of videos for businesses tend to be how-to videos and FAQ videos. These types of videos will allow you to show your subscribers how to use your products in the most effective manner. You can also show uses for your products that your customers may not be aware of. How-to and FAQ videos are also a great way to drive traffic to your website.

Sharing – When you create your YouTube channel, you will then be able to share your videos across your other social media pages. Posting your videos on your Facebook page is a great way to show your customers that you are on YouTube and that your videos have something to offer. You can also share links to your videos in your tweets, which will help expand your subscribers to your YouTube channel.

Feedback – Each time that you post a new video, you can gain valuable feedback. Your customers will be able to leave comments about your video, products, or tips that you included in your video. This is a great way for you to see what is working and what you may need to change.

Online Visibility – YouTube is also a great way for businesses to increase their online visibility. When someone searches for a product or service that you offer or have mentioned in a video, your link will be presented in those search results. To truly benefit from this, you should be sure to include relevant keywords in your video titles. This will help increase the visibility of your videos and gain valuable exposure for your business.

YouTube Stats

- 4 Billion Views a Day
- Each Second 1 Hour of Video is Uploaded
- Each Month there are 800 Million Users
- YouTube has had over 1 Trillion Views
- YouTube Mobile has 600 Million Views Each Day
- Google bought YouTube in 2006 for $1.65 Billion

Strategy #5: Mobile Marketing - One of the Newest Forms of Mass Marketing

Why is ***mobile marketing*** becoming so important? Well, let me ask you a question. Do you have a mobile device within arm's reach that you can access the Internet with? Go ahead. Think about it. I'll wait... Of course you do. Right now, within three feet of you, you probably have your cellphone. And that cellphone probably is a Smartphone... And that Smartphone has the ability to get online. You have a way of searching the web from nearly any mobile device.

When someone does a local search on a mobile device they usually make a purchase based on the information they find within 24 hours vs. a week or longer from a search on a computer. For restaurants it is usually within 60 minutes...

That is what we call a purchase driven consumer!

With *mobile marketing* there are a couple of ways to market information and there's also two ways to address the Google pending doom of Mobilegeddon for those who are NOT MOBILE READY. Let's first address the google issue that will result in massive lost in page ranking also known as *SEO* bleeding of profits.

Again I can just not stress enough on how much this new algorithm is going to impact your business. Especially if Panda or Penguin had an impact on you **ACT NOW!** Barry Schwartz on March 17, 2015 with Search Engine Land reported a quote:

"Google's Zineb Ait Bahajji is quoted as saying at SMX Munich the upcoming mobile-friendly algorithm will impact more sites than their Panda or Penguin algorithms."

Some people have the misconception that just because you may be able to pull up a website that looks like the desktop version they are mobile. They are not. In fact, if you look at a regular website on your iPhone or android, a lot of times they're jumbled up. The information or images can sometimes be stacked on top of each other.

Or if it does look the same online as the desktop, the screen is really small and you have to pinch and squeeze and move stuff around. And it's hard to navigate. (A key indicator that someone will bail if you make things difficult to get around.)

Mobile websites have been around now for a couple of years and the platforms that they were originally built upon are rather outdated to say the least. The latest technology that is frequently referred to as a mobile web site is actually called a *"Responsive Web Design."*

So what makes today's Responsive Web Design so much better?

Well for starters beyond being able to have the site automatically adjust to the viewing device because if its ease of functionality it allows a much greater conversion rate.

Another key component is the ability to segregate the interaction of devices and the user in split testing. This function is not available on the older platform. This marketing information can be pulled through the use of software like Clicktale or Optimizely creating a high-end type of heat mapping and A/B testing. You can literally see what is working or not in your marketing strategies and tactics. Raising your profit margins by information driven data.

Another fix that I like to refer to as a "Quick Fix" to stop the bleeding while you are working on your *responsive web design* is a *mobile site redirect.* Here this can take the concepts of putting the most important information above the fold on any device while granting an easy navigation for the most frequently asked questions and an option to be taken to the full site.

For instance, if it's a restaurant, it would have a contact us button, a menu button, a directions button, and maybe a specials button so that they can get to just the information that they're looking for. For example, for a restaurant website should have a takeout menu, because most people, when they go on their phone looking for food, it's takeout.

Doing this will help you in minimizing the ranking lost that is going to happen on April 21, 2015 and beyond. You can use the redesign to a *responsive web design* and use the mobile redirect as a quick fix.

This simple quick fix puts you leaps and bounds ahead of your competition who makes up excuses and chooses to do nothing. Their lack of action will result in bleeding profits while google ranks you higher just because you have a mobile friendly site even if it's just applying the quick fix to get started. Google will reward those who takes action.

Another way to utilize *mobile marketing* is with SMS or text messages. With text marketing, you have to first capture the subscriber's phone number and permission.

Then you can then market to them over time utilizing text messaging.

Why is mobile advertising so important? Well here's the thing: only about 36% of emails get opened compared to over 92% of text messages or mobile messages get looked at within the first minutes of being received. As a matter of fact, you've probably looked at your phone while you've been reading this report. That's the power of *mobile marketing*.

This high response rate of 92% in the text messaging area may be partially due to the sound notification. Even for those that do have the capability to have email sound notifications they tend to turn it off if they get more than 10 emails/day. However, text messages are more prone to be used as a more urgent or welcomed communication.

Using a Mobile App to Showcase Your Business

Yep... There's an app for that...

Today many local businesses are taking advantage of having an *app* made just for their business which is a *SMART MOVE!* Remember Google announce this is yet another way of getting ranked in the search engines as of February of 2015.

A mobile app is a software application developed specifically for use on a wireless device like a smartphone or tablet rather than a desktop or laptop computer. The applications are housed on and made available on Apple and Google Play.

A mobile app is a great way to engage in real-time with your customers. Maintaining a top of mind presence. It could be as simple as notifying them of a relevant and interesting blog post. Or other notifications that you have asked them ahead of time that they wanted details on such as certain webinar topics.

Let me share with you a few stats that reveals the importance of staying engaged with relevant communication. Some have referred to this as the 80-20 Rule where 20% of your efforts will create 80% of your results.

Let me show you what I mean:

Two % of sales are made on - first contact/touch
Three % of sales are made on - second contact/touch
Five % of sales are made on - third contact/touch
10 % of sales are made on - fourth contact/touch
80 % of sales are made on - fifth contact/touch!

However . . .

80% of Local Marketers give up after the first contact!

This could be due to the fact that they are using traditional marketing that is difficult to impossible to measure and costly to do manually. So out of frustration they move onto the next contact. Losing a potential gold mine had they developed a relationship instead.

As a business owner your greatest cost comes from acquiring your new customer. The least cost and greatest return on that initial investment is through engagement on a regular basis. A mobile app for your business gives your customers the opportunity to have your business information loaded directly on their smartphones so they can interact with your business and receive specific communications.

Having a customized app allows businesses to:

Build customer loyalty - Make your customers feel special by offering discounts, coupons, and promotions just for using your app.

Send push notifications - Deliver instant messages to your customers' mobile phones whenever you wish. While only 4% to 10% of emails get opened, push notifications get read 97% of the time.

Create viral buzz - Let customers quickly tell all of their friends about you using the built-in sharing capabilities of Facebook, Twitter, *LinkedIn*, your blog, SMS, and Email.

Grow your list - Gather names and email addresses directly inside your app and easily export them into your favorite email marketing campaign service.

Promote special events - Provide up-to-date information about all of your business events, sales, and promotions with an in-app events calendar that anyone can access.

Gain more credibility - These are still the early years of the mobile app. Having one adds serious credibility to your business—especially among those who don't know how easy we make it.

Keep customers informed - Fill your app with information about your business, service offerings, product samples, menus, and more. There's a tab for just about everything you want them to know.

Connect with ease - Make it simple for customers to reach you using one touch calling, email, a website link, and GPS directions to your business—all from inside your app

Get instant feedback - Allow customers to leave feedback on your fan wall, share photos, make restaurant reservations, and send comments in a variety of ways.

Track your success - Use robust analytics to track daily, weekly, and monthly downloads of your app.

Mobile Stats

- 50% of Consumers use their smart phones to find local businesses.
- Mobile Phones will be used more than PC's
- Over half of consumers use their phones in stores for buying decisions.
- In 1-year smartphones users will be over 1 billion worldwide.
- Mobile is predicted to be bigger than the Internet in 2 years.
- Over 70%+ of online retailers are developing a mobile strategy.
- Smart phone market is now bigger than the PC market.
- Over 60% of all searches are done on a smart-phone! Hence the reason behind the April 21, 2015 deadline for mobile ranking algorithm that was announced by Google directly for the deadline.
- As of April 21st mobile friendly will now be a factor in ranking your website over all.
- Serious of enough issue that Google sent out the first time ever through both email and web developer's tools notifications to web masters to fix the issues. Their algorithm will demote websites for mobile displaying and usability issues.

- So in essence, those who choose to not heed Google's warning and get mobile friendly even if they have poured thousands of dollars into their SEO marketing efforts on their desktop website their rankings will drop dramatically over night. Causing a major gash in their online presence and result in a bleeding of profits!

Strategy #6: Blogging - The Overlooked Local Marketing Tool

When most people think about blogging they think of a site focused on topics with a national scope. Locally focused blogs are powerful marketing tools for smart business owners. The power of the blog comes from the focus on the local community, which provides ample opportunities to use the city or town in the blog post headlines.

Blogs are very easy to create using one of the popular sites like Word Press or Blogger and with proper keyword placement the blog posts can easily rank on the first page of the search engines. Make sure your content has value to the audience you are trying to attract and be careful not to overload the posts with too many keywords. The example below shows a blog post ranking #1 for "Poor Cell Reception Florida" out of 6.6 Million results... and they say blogging isn't effective.

Always post a variety of content that your audience will find interesting. If you only post information about your business and products & services you will lose the interest of most readers.

Look for other local bloggers and offer them guest-posting opportunities on your blog. If Jay Leno were the only person on the Tonight Show it would eventually get boring... Jay is an entertaining guy but the guests on his show are what add the variety that keeps it interesting.

Use pictures and video on your blog. People are very visual in nature and a blog post with images and videos get more interaction than text only posts. Remember people want to be entertained and if they are looking for answers a picture can say a 1000 words to at least grab their attention. You can also name the picture files with the keyword to increase optimization for the post.

HOT TIP: Make the pictures stand out. The more bizarre the better. Try combining different images to grab attention. There's a lot of free services to help you do this.

Always ask for feedback. Engagement is very important with local audiences. Challenge your audience with questions and ask them to leave their answers and comments. This engagement will not only make things more interesting for the readers, it will also make the post more relevant to the search engines and you will be rewarded with better search rankings.

Direct Response Marketing - How to Get More Business Without Having to Get More Customers...

The fortune is in... The Fishbowl?

Not the thing you were expecting right? Think about it... you go into a restaurant and they have a fishbowl on the counter at the register for you to drop in a business card to enter to win a free appetizer, lunch, dessert, or maybe ever free drinks.

What do you think happens to those cards after they remove them from the **fishbowl?**

NOTHING!

I can tell you from experience.

At this point you may be thinking that's great but we don't have fishbowls on our front counter. And you are right...

But... EVERY business has a **fishbowl**, they just don't sit at the register and they don't look like fishbowls.

Remember the last time you went to the dentist or doctor and saw those client folders along the wall behind the receptionist with the colored tabs on them?

Fishbowl!

Ever go into a business that had rows of customer files in 4-drawer file cabinets along a wall?

Fishbowl!

Oil Change companies put that little sticker on your windshield...

Fishbowl!

Excel spreadsheets with customer invoices and contact info...

Fishbowl!

EVERY business that collects contact information from their customers has a Fishbowl! Those customers willingly gave you their information and it is your job...

your responsibility to tell them when you have an offer that they might find interesting.

Staying in touch with your customers is easier than you think!

There are very simple and inexpensive services called auto-responders that you can use to set up your client lists and send out communications to your customer base with the touch of a button. These systems can send email, text messages and some can even send recorded phone messages.

Email Marketing - Why an Automated Email System is Essential

These days, there are greater time constrictions on businesses which act to limit consistent marketing. Many of the limitations are due, in part, to fewer staff and tighter budgets. One of the greatest strategies to oppose this challenge is with the use of automated email systems for your business. These routine reminders are great for increasing website traffic and general sales.

Local businesses have seen tremendous results from this type of promotion and have abandoned antiquated and far more time consumptive methods of keeping in touch with clients. Understanding that workforce cutbacks and reduced line item funds for constant contacts are far more the norm than the exception, many companies have even eliminated them altogether.

If you find your company with staff that plays dual roles, you understand the importance of managing time and labor.

The controlled management of your sales process is crucial. An effective way of administrating this process is through maintenance with preset systems that contact your entire population. Many of these systems have tracking and progress reporting as a regular function. You can either go with an experienced company, or hire an IT professional to build an individualized program that best meets your center's needs.

There is a popular saying that declares, "...if you build it- they will come." It might be wise to add that if it is built and never used or disseminated, they will turn and go in another direction. Do not shoot your business success in the foot by making the mistake of inadequately using the system in which you invested. Make certain that the email addresses of all your clients are current. Have it be part of the process when they enter your business for scheduled visits. Check regularly to see which messages are returned and eliminate those addresses. It is encouraged to send out several reminders or informative messages. Your clients may not participate or purchase from the first contact, but they may just be ready when the next one arrives.

Build the opportunity for client suggestions and feedback into the message. Tag a staff member to be responsible for responding to the comments. These responses should be done in a timely manner. It could mean the difference between a happy customer and a lost one.

After you have had some time to track and monitor the impact of your businesses automated promotions system, don't just sit on the information. Take the time to let it guide and instruct your marketing future. Did it meet your contact needs? Did you see an increase to your website visits? Did you see an increase in visits to your physical location or the sale of a particular product? These strategies are not only save time and cost; they work to inform your marketing practices and processes. You will only enhance the good work and for which your center is known. You will also give your clients the consistent and careful service and information they deserve.

Some of my clients tell me that their customers are different... They say, "They don't want to hear from me after they buy my product." Until I share the following story with them...

An Unexpected Lesson in Follow-Up

In most places the government regulates power company operations. What that means is that you don't have a choice who you buy electricity from, you have to buy it from the company that has facilities in your area. They are referred to as "regulated monopolies".

This means that no matter how upset you get with the power company, you have to either buy electricity from them or not have any... Let's face it, there are usually only two instances where you even think about the power company, when you get your bill each month and when the lights go out. Neither one is what you would call a positive experience.

In 2003 there was one such company whose customer satisfaction scores were not horrible but they certainly were not great. Then disaster struck when they got slammed with two of the worst hurricane seasons on record. They had back-to-back-to-back hurricanes that left the majority of their customers without power for weeks.

Then, because they had exhausted their $1 Billion Dollar Storm Re-Building fund (power companies can't get insurance on their power lines) they had to go to their customers and tell them that we would have to charge them 10-15% more each month to replenish the fund.

To add insult to injury, the cost of fuel went through the roof during this same time frame and they had to increase their bills another 30% within a few short months.

Needless to say they had to deliver bad news to these customers over and over again during an 18-month stretch from August of 2004 to February of 2006. They were dreading the day that the customer satisfaction ratings would come out for the company.

The Shocking Truth

When they received their customer satisfaction scores they were blown away, the scores had improved to an all-time high!

It turns out that because they were communicating so regularly with their customers, that even though they were calling/emailing/faxing to give their customers bad news, the customer's perception of the quality of service actually went up!

As a result they developed a 12-point communication plan so that now they are touching base with each major account at least once a month. In the next year they actually won an award for being best in class for customer satisfaction. So much for "No news is good news"!

What does this have to do with your company?
Everything!

If customers who doesn't have a choice of who they buy a service from get a sense of high customer support from increased communications... How much more impactful do think it can be for your business! From my experiences it is substantial!

Just imagine how happy your customers will be when they receive a message from you that you are having a sale, offering a new service, a VIP program, prize give-a-ways, or just sharing a helpful tip on how to get more value out of your product of service. If it works for a big old power company it will work for you!

This is extremely important for service based industries. Because frankly, people tend to forget about the service details that they have. Even though they may continue to pay for a service for a number of months, usually the initial need which prompted the purchase is quickly addressed. So frequently, if they have not been reminded of the various services and benefit attributes they will eventually cancel.

This is especially true when money starts to get tight and they look for ways to cut cost. If they have not been using the service (not because they didn't need it but because they didn't know how to capitalize on their investment) they justify cutting the cost do to the lack of use. So it is very important to remind them via the other benefits that they could receive as well.

This issue could easily be addressed by giving examples of how else they could use the service using some sort of automated email service. You could focus on different examples at set time intervals.

HOT TIP: Look at your company's history, if you are tracking your numbers and you should be, you will see the tipping point so to speak that will reveal after so many years of being with the company when a customer tends to become a life-long user.
That is how you determine how far out you should set up different emails to keep them engaged in your service.

For example, if the company's history shows that they become a lifelong customer after five years you should plan on at least 70 monthly newsletters/emails after the first year. Each should reflect a different example to gain that long-term client.

Realize that during the first year you will need to have more frequent contact with your clients. Especially during the first four months then tapered a bit during months five to eight and then tapered again during months nine through 12.

This is also why learning how much your client is worth is so vital in your marketing strategy. You don't want to just sell them and leave them.

Bonus Strategy: Reputation Management – What Are They Saying About Your Online?

Many business owners fail to recognize how important their online reputation is. It can make the difference between increased sales and a dramatic drop in sales. Just one negative comment or review is enough to dramatically affect your online reputation. Once your reputation takes a hit, you will likely see decrease in website traffic and the amount of sales you would normally experience. Below you will find some ways in which you can monitor and manage your online reputation.

In order to see what potential clients see when they search for your business, simply perform a search as they would. This will show you what is being presented to searchers and what is being said about you and your business. Regularly monitoring your online reputation will ensure that if there is any negative content being published you are aware of it. If you know what is being said about you online, you are in a better position to take control of the situation and manage how the content is being seen.

During your research, if you notice any negative post or comment that has been published regarding your business you should act quickly to minimize any negative effect it may have. One negative comment can be enough to cost you potential clients. No matter how hard we try as business owners, we have to realize that we cannot please everyone 100% of the time.

If you notice a negative post on any of your social media pages, you should address that comment immediately. The quicker you act to remedy the situation the less likely the unhappy customer will be to post any additional comments. If you choose to ignore the comment and not reply, the individual may continue to post additional comments, which can have a dramatically negative effect on your online reputation.

The key is to act quickly and do everything within your power to solve the problem.

Taking a proactive approach to your online reputation can provide you with valuable insight into the type of content being published about your business and brand. The more involved you are in the process the easier it will be to notice any newly published negative content. Once you are aware of this content, the key is to act quickly and decisively. This will ensure that the negative content is taken care of and any further searches will present people with positive reviews and content.

There is nothing that can damage a business more than negative comments being posted online. However, if you are proactive and continue to monitor your online reputation, you will be better prepared to deal with these situations as they occur.

A Word On Branding

Properly branding your new business is one of the most important steps you can take on your way to successfully marketing your local business. Establishing your brand will inform potential clients of what your business does and who you are.

One of the most important elements of your brand is your logo. It is what will become the face of your company and what people will associate with you and your business. Having consistency across all the platforms and strategies we have discussed is essential to portray a congruent brand.

When you properly brand your business, you will be able to set yourself apart from your competitors. Your business is unique, and it should be branded as such. This will also allow you to reach your target audience more effectively and create marketing plans centered on your brand. When properly implemented, a successful marketing plan will help you reach your target audience. This means those who can truly benefit from your particular products and services will hear your message.

Branding your business will also help you create an emotional connection with clients. When you emotionally connect with your clients, you will create a way in which they can identify and connect with your business. This can be achieved through the use of a well-designed logo and marketing plan. Your logo is what will identify your business; because of this the design should be something that is recognizable as your brand and identifies your business.

A well-established brand is also an effective way to create trust in your target market. If potential clients believe that you are a trustworthy business, they are more likely to purchase your products and services. A business that is properly branded will experience a greater response from their emails, advertisements, and newsletters. As more people become invested in your brand, they will be more confident in the products and services that you offer. This trust can then translate to an increased amount of website traffic and sales.

When you're creating your brand, you should focus on the long-term goals of your business. Your brand is not something that is only being created to serve a short-term goal. The brand that you build should be strong enough to last through expansions and time while remaining consistent. This is the long-term marketing technique that appeals to audiences now and in the future.

Your brand should be designed to enhance your business, while adding a sense of permanence and reliability to your business. Your brand is what will be used to identify you now and in the years to come; because of this, it should be something that will instill trust in the minds of your clients today and in the future.

Special Report Content: The 11 Essentials to Marketing Your Business Online

With the countless methods of promotion being enlisted in today's market, it is vital to make sure that your company stays in step. Marketing your business online takes planning, commitment and the decision to use the tools wisely. Here are 11 Essentials to keep in mind as you begin:

Essential 1

Before you begin your campaign, take time to carefully plan a strategy. What is your goal? What do you plan to gain? How much time can the company devote to research and analysis? One surefire plan is to start with the basics and grow from there.

Essential 2

Make certain that your website and contact information on all web searches are kept current. Check all links and backlinks to make sure that they are validated and functioning. Remove any that aren't working to ensure that you get constant traffic, unhindered by bugs.

Essential 3

Treat your online plan and the maintenance as a legitimate department. Have 'department meetings' on a regular basis to appropriately monitor data and make needed adjustments. Assuming that automations and follow-ups will happen on their own will cause huge mistakes and could create missteps and missed opportunities.

Essential 4

Keep consistent in your contact. Make sure that the clients hear from you. Share the most pertinent information about your business and any important dates. Share your business success stories and new changes that may be on the horizon. This can easily be done using *LinkedIn*.

Essential 5

Make sure that your company's mission is always kept in the forefront. Test all content and other writings against it to ensure that they are aligned. Make sure that anyone you contract any of your marketing services to is also very aware of your mission. Have an approval process for content before it is allowed to be posted.

Essential 6

Use social media. Good news travels fast, but bad news travels faster. Make sure that the messages and social connection opportunities are a positive reflection of your business by finding clients who are willing to write positive reviews and comments on pages like *LinkedIn*, Facebook and Google +.

Essential 7

Join a forum and create a blog that is geared specifically toward that audience for your business. Create a niche and use it often. The more visible your company is, the more traffic you get and the greater your connections and earning potential can be.

Another idea is to create a group in which you are the leader who can add or delete members. This can be done in both FaceBook and *LinkedIn*. Again constantly bring value and they will keep coming back. This social approach grants you "Social Proof" that you can in turn use in your marketing efforts especially in webinars.

Essential 8

Make sure that your clients have a venue available that allows them to give feedback and suggestions. They will feel heard and become loyal to your company and your brand.

Essential 9

Program any of your client contact systems to key in on special dates like customer birthdays, the anniversary of them first visiting your company. The options for specialization are many. This, too, will build greater confidence in your business.

Essential 10

Make sure that your entire staff is involved and that they share their stories mission with the same vigor and enthusiasm that you would; communication is key.

Essential 11

Don't let inactivity and outdated content destroy your hard work or your reputation. If it isn't relevant, delete it.

Turbo Boost Your Results - Invitation

By now you have the principles and techniques to quickly grow your business. If you would like to expedite the marketing process explained in this book you can visit EnhanceYour.Net and we will help dominate your local market and establish you and your business as the expert in your area. You can also visit our website and register for an in depth marketing analysis.

I also invite you to learn more on how to maximize your networking efforts in the professional arena using **LinkedIn**. So that you can truly take advantage of its power that most are not aware of or uncertain on how to tap into it.

I am a firm believer that any and all activities should have a purpose and with a positive return on investment (ROI) be it in time or money. Especially in time, which is the one commodity that cannot be replaced.

Let me take you by the hand and show you through a three part series *LinkedIn* video training program. Where I demonstrate how to fulfill and turbo boost your marketing efforts addressed in this book under the Essential categories 4, 6, and 7.

This training can be found at the following link:

SmartAction.info/Brand-Yourself-LinkedIn-Training-Series

By now, you have been informed and understand the importance of having a ***responsive mobile website*** that can create a positive user experience through both display and ease of usability.

With images and content automatically adjusting in size across all devices it is in your best interest to invest in a ***responsive mobile website***. Even if you have built a $10,000 website a few years ago the technology is outdated and you don't want to lose traction in the *SEO* efforts you have done up to this point.

Remember April 21, 2015 is the Google deadline before "Mobilegeddon" - Google's Impending Doom On All Sites That Are Not Mobile Optimized happens. This new algorithm surpasses Google's previously established guidelines for ranking. Don't get left behind!

Also remember the primary function of **mobile website** aka **responsive web design** is to draw in your target market. Using the power of a search engine like Google to direct them.

A mobile redirect is a good "Quick Fix" to help minimize the loss of your SEO investment up to this point on your desktop website.

A ***mobile app (which as a reminder is another means to rank the site)*** is to help engage your target market by keeping you on top of mind before, during and after the initial purchase or engagement. It creates a desire to keep them wanting to come back and share the love about you or your company.

Go to **EnhanceYour.Net** _now_ and _enroll_ in our newsletter to get great content that you can apply right now of what is working in _TODAY'S_ market. Keep your finger on the marketing pulse. Get better ROI in your marketing efforts and a positive business experience for your clients and potential clients.